The Heat Yesterday

The Heat Yesterday

Ian Iqbal Rashid

Coach House Press
Toronto

Coach House Press
760 Bathurst Street, 2nd floor
Toronto, Canada
M5S 2R6

© Ian Rashid, 1995

FIRST EDITION
1 3 5 7 9 8 6 4 2
Printed in Canada

Published with the assistance of the Canada Council, the Department of
Canadian Heritage and the Ontario Arts Council.

Cover illustration: Stephen Andrews
Author photograph: Liane Harris
Cover design: Shari Spier / Reactor

Canadian Cataloguing in Publication Data

Rashid, Ian Iqbal
The Heat Yesterday

Poems.
ISBN 0-88910-483-2

I. Title

PS8585.A79H43 1995   C811'.54   C95-931950-6
PR9199.3.R38H43 1995

For Peter

Contents

You Are What You Were,
You Are What You Were

Remember Who You Are,
Remember Where We Were

Song of Sabu [1]

1.

I was born under a Banyan tree. Later I was found. Discovered. *A little devil with a wonderful smile.* Junglee, then a jungle boy. Then a star. I am the most famous Indian in all of the movies. Still. I was chosen.

A star. The audiences loved me. *Action,* and I would bring on that thin-skinned feeling. Pull in words by their tails. They chose me.

They chose me, they loved me. Men who love only women remarked on the beauty of my body. My skin. Rich and wet like mud in the studio heat. And such dark eyes, they said. Dark and runny but with surprise. An underground lagoon. The edgeless shimmer of my hair. On and on and on in the lights. Floating. Without borders.

I loved my countries. India made me.
America made me famous. They ask
me to choose which. Who chooses? Me?
I cannot. The better question: who
chooses me?

And England. I have fought only for
God's countries in my films. Pride and
tears. And in my life: have I told you I
have medals? That my father died in
service? Let them say anything against
my countries—anything—and I will
square my shoulders like the stack of
filing cards in my agent's office. I will
stare and stare. Some fear I might blind
them with my stare. When I look back.
Little devil with a wonderful smile. But I
can look back. Sometimes, my heart
beats so fast, so loud. Its echo bounces
through my insides until it rests on my
tongue. Now: feel my belly, feel behind
my ribs. That's fear.

3.

I was famous. The starlets held my arm for photographs. You can still find them. Twos of us, smiling. In special motion-less circles of air in which we will always live.

The pretty, pretty girls who scrunched their noses in delight whenever I spoke. My sing-song words spraying their faces. Cheeks caressed on a breath of fruity beer and sandalwood.

Later some would stay with me. Sometimes and for a while. Hang over me and descend. Then their muscles would clench. As if they could not trust their weight upon the darkness on which they rested.

And sometimes it was me. Amazed. Chosen. Lying rifle-straight on top. As if a flag were planted in the shaft of my spine.

Then it ended. Now I wake up each
morning already defeated by the day.
The films began to sneer at me. I did
not choose them. They were ugly and
cranking as if I were the only human
being in a jumble of monsters and
machinery. Not chosen. Convenient.
Soon not even that.

I have always preferred reincarnation to
heaven. More surprises. But here I am.
In a wood-paneled heaven. My wife is
still lovely, they tell me. Sometimes I
have an urge. To trap her as she stands
there under a bell-shaped glass. Her hair
piled up, her eyes looking down. Glass
might make her look shiny again, make
her dull white skin gleam. I want to trap
her until I am collected. Until I know
what to say.

I break things. I do. I used to bound onto
hippopotamuses. Leap into tall purple
jungles. But now my joints need oiling.

I break things and she does everything gingerly, from memory, with her saw-dust-covered fingers. My American wife. And my children in their thoughtless lives. They cut through everything I say. Nowadays everything I say is attached to other things, to words I've spoken before. Attached by long strands of milky film which my children tear through, leave in shreds, picking up only what serves them. My American children who are unbreakable. Chosen.

5.

The night time frightens me. My only
comfort is the taste of cocoa after tears.
The bitter liquid cutting through the
feel of glue in the back of my throat. I
keep the taste in memory after the last
few drops. I'm afraid to sleep. I dream of
the circus. Mean elephants and glower-
ing clowns. I'm afraid to make more
cocoa. I break things.

Sometimes during the day I catch myself
in the mirror. The carelessly put togeth-
er beauty found in young boys. But day
time ghosts—they're easily dealt with.

Mango Boy

1.

Maple syrup on mango
                    works, you are
A Canadian child
I'm told.

And so
        I dunk it all in yogurt
                pour cardamom
                        and pistachio
(yes, some mint)
                        whip it up defiant,
One clove.
                        Cinnamon.

In London, the seat of empire
(underwear showing through now)
I eat mangoes, sliced
see the cayenne
sprinkled, machine-gunned through honey-coloured
flesh.

Then I ride my lover high
and marvel at my fortune:
this projection screen of back
so white and vacant, so long
able to hold so many of my moments
Saturated, I arch
onto waxy shine of bum
shot through with pimples and pink
moments of blush and   teeth marks
remembering a mango splintered smile.

I need a name we all need a name
I'll take back my second
or maybe just speed it up past my first
or maybe call myself something new
that will make people angry:
Shabani or Pierre Elliot or Giles
or Mango Boy

I'll grow over-ripe mango messy-lazy
offend like an unremovable stain
mango legacies, mango regrets

Live up to a new reputation
Expensive, but I peel for free
I'll make propositions, like:
like try me in the water, no mess in the water
            or
squeeze the mango boy and watch
it
all
comes
out   then
then think of a name   then
then tell me

Barbie's New Home

1.

Barbie is unhappy. She knows her rights. She knows what was hers to expect and enjoy. A house, grand and uneventful. Predictable. Barbie would have been happy there. A house flashing with laughter and mirrors, burdened only by big armchairs and oversized cushions for her hard little bottom. Burdened only by last year's colours. But Barbie wouldn't have minded. She's polite that way.

Big floppy flowers that last and last and last. Like daytime in the summer, Barbie knows what to expect. But look at what has happened. *Things aren't the way they used to be.* Change. Barbie has been thrown into the face of change, like a petal into a big wind.

2.

Dark and smiling and noisy. Very dark. This family is very different from Barbie. Different even from Malibu Barbie, Barbie's relentlessly tanned alter-ego. This family is darker still. A house full of mocha coloured children, all very different from Barbie.

But then all children are different from Barbie. They don't enter the world fully formed like she does. Little globes of cobalt blue knowing for eyes. A little whim of a nose. Children change all the time. Grow and change, develop spots and unfortunate pendulous breasts, or worse still, no breasts at all: those little girls who demand brassieres and waste money. And the big ones who refuse them, costing nobody anything. Except modesty. And who profits from a lack of modesty? Barbie's breasts on the other hand do have a price. Envy. Envy and twenty-nine ninety-nine.

3.

Barbie's new friend is a boy.
(Barbie never has owners, only
"friends", she is built that way.)
And even more unusual, he's
a little brown boy. No chance
for envy here. Or is there?
Something splits the air when
his big cow eyes look her way.
Barbie stares back at him, her
gaze steadily forward, her smile
gripped into place by a round of
determination in her cheek (do
her nerves show?). Barbie stares
steadily forward. She longs for
eyelids.

At night he holds her to him
with love. She is as close to his
mouth as saliva and she is fright-
ened. She doesn't recognise this.
She knows what men are, their
inevitability, it's been built into
her. By men themselves. But this
boy is different.

Men are supposed to be dark. *Tall, dark and handsome.* But this dark? And everything is exposed in this boy. Where are the shrewd eyes, the lecher's mouth? Where are those pretty cotton candy words, the smiles with their did-I-see-them moments of dislike, ebbing into speculation, flowing into promise. Barbie knows what she knows. And she knows what to expect. This ... this is something else.

Everywhere the smell of curry
and hope. Hope permeates the
air like a scent's source beyond
view. The child plays with eager
fervour. Barbie's roles are not
unfamiliar: movie star, spy, stew-
ardess—oops, flight attendant—
but such elaborate fantasies, no
easy narratives here. Plots from
old films, dancing and singing
numbers (so many languages)
and then, even worse ...
Twisted, shapeless romances.
Unrequited love stories. Barbie
feels miscast. Not a wedding in
sight. (A shame. Barbie arrived
with a full-length gown made
from synthetic lace—highly
flammable, but children shouldn't
be playing with matches, should
they?) Barbie knows only to be
Barbie. To be dressed swiftly,
propped up, *to twirl.* This is so
much different.

The boy's sweat glands are beginning to change. Curry and hope and a man's sweat. Barbie knows only to be Barbie; she's not up to much more. She has always been grateful for her lack of genitalia, no smelly orifices to confuse her. She is grateful now. She remembers to smile with even greater urgency.

I know what I know, she thinks.

Barbie is concerned about her lit-
tle fashion purse, and her little
mini dress. She is being carried
from room to room, naked. No
purse, no dress. She is more than
concerned (dark eyes surround
her). The fashion earrings that
she has been given are wrong.
Meant for someone else. A differ-
ent outfit, some other girl.
Hoops as big as slave bands, flash
a lethal light across the dark
walls. If she could perspire,
Barbie decides, she would now.
She must leave this place.

6.

Hope and exercise, plans for improved status. Life here is unified and hard-headed, exhausted eyes and tough feet. Barbie wants out. She is plotting. A tight-lipped, pink-faced girl comes to visit the big-eyed boy. They play all the wrong games but Barbie is aware of being stared at hard and with envy. Sneaky eyes which Barbie recognises. Oh, she knows this girl. There is something here she can work with. She will not have to wait long. Soon, she'll be whisked out. Leave behind a trace of her cool, slick surface and the smell of marigolds. And a brief, tearing sensation that will last long after she has been stolen away into a peppermint-scented pocket and secreted down a stairwell. Barbie knows what she knows. And that is all.

Market Tavern

1.

Scrawny carcass of a South London bar. Too sober to dance on the lip, shuffling in the bowels instead, waiting to restart my heart. My closed eyes hidden—I'm trying to perk up my buzz. Movements, slight movements from my groin, little sweeps of motion, asides, moments skinny as parentheses.

Arms all around, fork for my attention, slicing the rank from above, circling, flicking the glisten off my head. I think of Tippi Hendren for a second. Then a joke about fucking Hitchcock. Two seconds pass.

A song from thirty years ago, souped up, now placed on a motorcycle. I'm moving now, picking up my shuffle, elbows angled a few degrees higher.

2.

My mother was young in London once, a honey coloured
girl. Never danced, she refused to dance. Dreaming of mar-
riage, to Englishmen (who wouldn't look back). But also
dreaming of home, a place where there was no cold. A place
that would only refuse her now: *gone foreign, loose woman,
what have they taught her over there* ...

She could tell them of adding machines and shorthand, of
bed-sits and memorising running routes home, should
attentions—a kiss—be demanded (but dreaming of a kiss,
dry, dry kisses only, no tongues, no mess) or a dance (but
dreaming of a dance, memorising every step to dream later,
every word of every song—she can even dream in them
today).

3.

Now my mother's son so far from home—home a place that is so rarely warm—finds a hand white as fear on his crotch. Hand moves up, lifts my shirt, finds my brown belly tattooed laser yellow and stays, absorbing the changes in colour.

Spread fingers search for an outline, every hair counted along the way as fingers move upward to my throat.

I stop moving, not afraid, just stunned by the possibilities of such heat from fingertips.

No dreams for me. Tonight, I'll sleep hard and long and empty.

Bastards of the Diaspora

for Himani Bannerji

1.

... we realise that our migrations did not take us where they should have, that our refuges have betrayed us ... But there is not much point in saying that one does not belong. Merely in assuming that belonging only means a happy positivity ...
—HIMANI BANNERJI

My father is evaluating his life on the drive home from work. Suddenly he smells change as he steps on the freeway. Things have rearranged themselves, he thinks. *What has changed?* He looks at his reflection in the rear-view mirror. *Grey.* But he is not old. *Labour and grief.* He begins to drive faster. Confusion. *Home.* He leaves his car thinking he can trust his feet. *Earth.* He takes himself by the hand as he turns the final street-corner. *Allah.* He has been betrayed. Swamped with familiarity: *My God, I am home.*

Anger and anguish and a rush of loss. *I am home.* His knees leave him as if he was dying in a dream. A legless fall into the dark. But that jolt of gravity, to wake. Where is it? *This is home.* To know there is hope, another morning and that he is not truly ...

2.

... It is since colonisation, and now recolonisation, under a siege of cultural imperialism and racism, that we find an intense upsurge of cultural politics. This politics of being, essentialising or fixing who we are ...

—HIMANI BANNERJI

Moral regulations in the wake of a swirl of fabric. *If you are Muslim, you can not be what your are,* she says her sari falling into perfect lines around her as she moves. How can her certainty wound me so much? Me, manoeuvring in my bigger world, such a big world. She looks at me, monitoring the surprise she has launched onto my features. Her peacock dome retracts slightly, a corner of fabric drapes and drops, becomes wired around the corner of her ear. She waits. There is so much silence. I can hear our watches are out of synch.

I suddenly know what to say. *You were not this when we met before, in another place.* The surprise is returned. She has heard all the questions before but this one. She recovers her head, moves forward, whether to jostle or embrace oblivion, I cannot be sure. I hear the charge of fabric as she walks by me. But the rustle whispers to me: *survival.* My indignation tramples over me in retreat. *Sssssurvival.*

3.

… What makes us think that an existence in any given moment is anything but authentic?

—HIMANI BANNERJI

My brother cannot speak any other languages? *Just English.* Smirks of amusement. *Don't need any others. Born and raised in Toronto. Live in Toronto. Might go to Ecuador for a while. Oh, I've got Spanish, but that's not what you mean, is it?* Suddenly the words are heavy. Hard to push each one across the space that has appeared. That separates his world from theirs.

At night he dreams of a carnival draped in silks, a carnival crier bellowing out in Hindi. There is a desperation in this voice, as it parades the grounds, calling out my brother's name. But my brother hears nothing menacing so he announces his arrival. He is ushered through the doors of the Bharat hall of mirrors, *find your authentic reflection among the bastards!*, which lock behind him. The voice begins to laugh, to frighten him—*Did you know it was possible to laugh in Hindi?*—mocking.

And my brother wakes slippery into the tangerine morning.

As the carnival fights back, making one last effort to hold him. But in just a few moments, dissatisfied, it will stretch itself, shrug in today's light and be gone.

All this new love of my parents' coun-
tries. We have bought the videotapes
together, bought the magazines and
books, all the advertisements, clothes,
and each others' responses. We watch
the slides of your visit. Your handsome
face is tanned surrounded by mango
trees, planted above the poverty. The
moist beauty—which you think of
blowing up and then framing, building
into your walls—majesty imposed upon
majesty.

Now I watch you watch Sergeant
Merrick watch poor Hari Kumar. And
follow as the white man's desire is twist-
ed, manipulated into a brutal beating.
You are affected by the actor's brown
sweating body, supple under punish-
ment. What moves you? The pain with-
in the geometry of the body bent? The
dignity willed in the motions of refusal?
A private fantasy promised, exploding
within every bead of sweat? Or is it the
knowledge of later: how my body will
become supple for you, will curve and
bow to your wishes as yours can never
quite bend to mine. What moves you
then?

My beauty is branded into the colour of
my skin, my strands of hair thick as
snakes, damp with the lushness of all
the tropics. My humble penis cheated by
the imperial wealth of yours: Hari's cor-
poral punishment, mine corporeal. Yet
this is also part of my desire. Even
stroking myself against your absence, I
close my eyes and think of England.

Knowing Your Place

1. *Passage from Africa / A Pass to India*

i)

I know these places awkwardly
like the bundles I take with me
that soon I hope
will float beside me constantly.

These places are sudden
with absence of metaphor.
Like the absences my parents live with:
an ebbing of fluency
a poverty of words for white
unable to dream in snow.

ii)

They were sent to a place without light.
Home is *the dark continent.*
An immovable mass keeping us separate
blocking the view between our stories.

Did they leave
as I leave now
carrying papers
in case they might vanish?

iii)

Vanish and merge
emerging as people we've never known, unfinished.
Like stories with disappeared endings
told by old photos and older women
bent by time and disapproval.

Stories fading
at their salt water edges
curling, crisp with hints.

iv)

Stories which hold me often
whose endings
like fists are snake-tight
over-eager embraces
that open to caress me, now and again

now, mocking my obsession
this open hand of a story
its teasing misshapen fingertip of a subcontinent.

And I leave
reading one of two epic poems
governing a struggle
that will not vanish

gripping a line
that zips open a sky of myth
exposing its soft
little boy's belly

leaving stiff vestments behind,
leaving an anger behind
with the buildings we are tunneling by with a roar

leaving for a place that knows me well
    as a cell
        under attack
            knows its virus.

2. *Goa*

Places: know
that there are no
more in the world to know

skilled, you have seen them all
predicted them
worn them eaten them touched ...
                    paid
        sounded
each one held then tallied
all held in your tale   you tell
of taking it all in—foreignness,
in strange rooms for four
circus coloured walls coming in on you
blown in by imported breezes
plump with spice   which you know

it was told to you by a shell
the complexity of cardamom
held in one nostril then picked
pinned and fixed on a map
panorama, from faraway to around the corner
all known adding weight to your skin
all seen through your inky gaze
arranged by a pen and a stamp
known: sureness of syntax
sentimental shorelines   shells
no more threatening than a flabby belly

3. *Scottish Highlands*

I know
that there are no
more places
to know

only skills
to imagine
sheep coloured
houses

or practice
streaks of Rajasthani
red into sky
blue of seas,

swing familiarity
into sinewy bridge
over waves

of muscular
shoulders in mountain,
idle flexes lingering
in surprise

of valleys

known?

I must have

rehearsed my gasp
against violent dance-step
of sharp bend
in road

then all sudden flat
I must have known
this choreography of grass
in advance

This drive to nature confounds me. On the one hand—and I spread it against the car window, watch the New World through hand-made geese formations—I am ill-tempered pretending to read, afraid of the electricity threatening the air, threatening the brittle balance with the new, the harshness of white woods, the kindness of strangers who brought me here.

Why this flash of nerves? The darkening skies do not hoard magic, are too comprehensible. But still sudden change, the quiver of light and shade, spoil my peripheral vision, unmood me.

On the other hand—now a trapped brown on glassy purple grey of sky, purple green of tree— this nature reminds me holds me unables me to claim this. Brownness on glass paints my nature urban. *Pakis live in suburbs, pakis live in ghettos.* Brown thumb and forefinger cup all that is visible. Contradictions, so much distance measured in the span of one hand.

The Memory of Fingertips

for my grandmother

1.

Her life got by our clamour, our urgent building,
like the narrowest little river slips through a city.

I have a photograph of her gazing at a departure
(perhaps my own) as if it were a horizon. (*A hori-
zon is a lie*, I learned later.) It was a time of leav-
ings, of sadness. A time of resignation as she was
left behind. But there is an alert stillness that I see
in the photos now, a tension found in explorers
about to begin their own journeys. She was leav-
ing, going someplace without me. And there was
no sadness there, not exactly, just *how to find a
way to say good-bye?*

Photographs: that last one with her arms folded, like she was just about to step back inside (even though we were inside, at Eaton's). Her chapped lips seem to tear apart rather than separate, her eyes show an underlay of gold, like sunlight through brown water. How strange she looks, in front of that photographer's fancy backdrop— the humble faded presence of someone known, someone from home.

Then there are the other pictures: a tiny, sickle shaped girl, her head covered. Pretty, vivid, the one you looked at first. More and more pictures, scattered moments attempting to sum up a life. Her faces dissolve and reappear, new selves take shape, rising up to me in degrees, becoming solid. But I know her true face, her final face. The one she was aiming for, the one that wasn't photographed. All hollow and sharpened—a stark, bare shaving of grey.

Why is this mourning not dangerously slivered? Why no rush toward forgetfulness, that hurried leap past grief? That need to say good-bye with so much feeling that your voice breaks.

3

Our home is a melting smell she would say and I feel something clench inside her like a deep, internal grip. *Wild oceans swept up to the places we called home.* What must she think of my home, I wonder? A thin city propped up on a lake as flat and pale as paper. Or in the winter: an arty scrawl against white.

We leave one morning for the doctor's. I make her go back to change, find something to keep her legs warm. (Nothing about the hard bright light told her it would be cold.) She returns with her legs encased in white nylon stockings beneath her skirt. The wind blows hard, occasionally revealing a frosty sheen like the bloom on a plum.

Back home everything she touched moved off in galloping directions. All her gestures roped in with confidence. The move to every word certain, not yet bridled by English. And now she creaks forward in jagged diagonals, I think, unsure as she clasps my hand.

But at the doctor's, after hours of searching, for words that defy translation, for ailments that can't be located, when I ask her to end a complicated form with an "x", a smile appears like a lightening rod. She winks and offers the surprise of a signature. I expect a gnarled crumple—but her names, when they come, are rounded and curly: balloons anchored at magical angles to one another.

4.

What did she make of the century's transforma-
tions? What did she make of her own?

I think now of those science-class words, words
that meant absence of movement, paralysis.
People stayed where they were.

During a later visit she reaches up to tousle my
hair, but I am not there the way she remembers.
Her fingertips want hair falling softly over eyes, a
long thickness, a soft sheen that she wants to
press with her palm. She is remembering a boy
who lurched among chair legs like a brightly
coloured top. A boy who aroused bearded chuck-
les and crinkled scolding.

On the phone, over the crackle of a bad line she
tells me to come home and visit her. (*Home,* she
said.) That she no longer remembers who to pic-
ture when she speaks to me. *Home,* she said, and
people stayed where they were.

What did she make of my movements, my
crowded life hurtling forward, too unstable for
her to climb onto. How was she able to confirm
my outline in the blur, to hold me, to ease pain
she couldn't even name? Appearing from
behind gauze curtains that look like bandages she
would know I was awake, just from the bated
quality to the air, a clumsy adult man feigning
sleep. How did she manage that thin sweet tone-
less hum no louder than a purr, to place comfort
beside me like the curl of a warm cat. To softly

shut the door behind her with such care that
every hinge, every part of the latch creaked a
whispered *I know.*

Her room seems drained of colour as if it has already slipped into the dimmest reaches of memory. Even outside, the buildings are so faded they seem hand-tinted.

Death had pushed her hard in the end. Like waves that had rolled her forward, one wave after another, coming closer and closer together. These deaths never left her, *what kind of mother outlives her children,* but finally allowed her to balance on a narrow surface, allowed her to live there inches above the sadness.

I sit here like she must have done, pressing fingertips to lips. The plaintive wail of a Hindi film song is trampled by the outside traffic. Inside, the elaborate filling of white hours, the glad pounce upon the most inconsequential task. Oceans of chatter and photographs eddy around us.

That was the song that played at my sister's wedding in 1963, someone says. *And she wore that sweater when she came to Canada, I sent it to her from England in 19 ... It must have been 1971.* Gloves. Her hands were badly callused, probably for most of her life. *I remember them against my fevered forehead, her cool and definite fingertips.* Fingertips. How to live free in a world where the passing of time holds such power.

You Are What You Were,
You Are What You Were

Returning to Canada

I arrive again, my returns timed like coincidences.
Immediately, I cock my kindness like knobby
wings, and cluck too much.

All day your house is dark, drapes closed. A crack
of light cuts through the velvet feeling, trans-
forms the dust in the air into a sparkling chande-
lier. And the house is full of visitors—they sit
quiet in chairs at appalled angles to each other.
Every now and again, we rise suddenly, cup your
few words like raindrops in a drought.

Your white face becomes shadowed by a violet
colour of night under your eyes and I put you to
sleep. I am waiting to remove my clown's smile,
muscles tired from all the faces I have made. The
only sounds now are an occasional rattle: my tired
natter and the bottles half-filled with pills that I
feed you—bottles with choppy, energetic names
on them like sounds from another language.

Downstairs, I finally think I hear you sleeping,
my every tendon tense between each of your long
slow breaths. I imagine a rectangle cutting
through the ceiling, your stark bones lying per-
pendicular to the beams of the attic.

I still feel this thing for you—a longing that caus-
es my insides to lurch as if I had leaned out over
a cliff. I wake up trying to remember, knowing I
have dreamed some possibility that I had never
before considered.

Third Nipple

Remembering that last summer can peel a mind raw. We all rented a little four-room shotgun house in an ugly jewel-named town. No one in that town slept. Neither did we. The nights were full of metallic-shaped drives and gun-metal skies. And the cramped sprawl of books and unfinished papers and ordinary shells brought back from the beach and uncleared plates and the hair dryer on the bookshelf. And an ever-tracing fin-gertip—someone's video camera— never quite touched it. Only wagged happy at shadows—an inside-out ghost story. And that's where the story ends, I guess, with the video.

The camera galumphs away from me on the phone—clutching a salty smelling receiver—over to you across the room on a keyboard. Your wrists are arched, angled high. It's only the delicacy of your touch—not the broken microphone—that keeps the image silent. We're all having a party. Late summer drunk munching on popcorn. Sieved-through-the-ceiling heat drizzles a clarified butter over us. Your shirt is off strategically for the camera which only wants your face—handsome—disguised by a lop-sided shy. What we can't see is a lesion that has positioned itself perfectly between your nipples. That's for much later rememberings and careful shaking of heads.

You Are What You Were

1. You Are What You Were

I had almost learned to forget them all

The dry
grassy-smelling boys
glistening

old fashioned handsome
like vintage cars
all muscle and rounded, honking

shiny hooded eyes
that became wild later, shouting
on streets at the dead-makers

lean and synchronised
one side of a camel in motion
forgotten

but for the surprise of skin
flaking to touch, translucent
hair smelling of months

and months of body
in fever, just
a sweet smell is all

I might remember
of the dry
grassy-smelling boys

2. *Dead Optimism*

Grim line
of mouth
behind admissions
asks

how much
and how long
you've been bleeding
I'm relieved

there are degrees
things
could
be
worse

I sit in the waiting room
waiting
among the other clenched fists
my breath becoming
metallic smells of Coca-Cola

I have been monitoring
my love growing so pale, flawed
cowardly

this is why I sit here
elbowed by the blows
of *please*

      please
please   this is why I lie
between sips of Coca-Cola
why I say I don't remember my dreams

3. *Ordinary*

I remember
how you used to tease me

scold me
for my youth
and carelessness

somehow it has switched
and I've become
the clever one

(I don't remember
that moment
of equal
when it was neutral

where was I)
responsible
carefully measuring
sustenances

feeding
you my measured
sympathies
I remember

feeling
              special
I forget how
extraordinary

illness has made me
so thick and solid

ordinary
everything ordinary
except for
your oily gazes

and splatter-gun
observations
which splash
hard

between my eyes:
you say: *it's like your hand's
gone to sleep*
as you touch my soiled, rubber-
gloved hand *or*
like
you're dead

4. *Now What Did I Come in Here For?*

You drifted
into melancholia
so gradually

that I didn't even notice

—a slow
disappearing act—
until the only things left
are sheets

hardened
like hillocks on the bed
frozen
landscapes as you enter

forgetting
what are you there for?
all you have are clues
gestures, a flick of the wrist
or a pushing or pulling of arms
motions like pantomime

repeated

until the dead awaken
force a realisation

sheets
can be left
unchanged if you want
forever   gestures
don't need completion

5. *Memorial Service*

I am still
embarrassed
at memorial
services

never able to
forget
myself   uncomfortable
with failure

but at this one
there's a photo
of you in a white shaggy
wig

you look
like a coconut
cake

flaking
skin part
of your
camouflage

and when
the people sing
they slowly
fill

the building
like
water
first murmuring and splashy

then gliding
over space
to form one single level surface

6. *Two Marches*

it's scary
today
can't decipher style
skin the only costume

now muscles
and fat spill, spell
significance

bare arm transports tattoo
and shoulder drills
back of neck

back of neck
is a treacherous memory

we march wall to wall then
down Church St. *what do we want*

your neck
smell of sunburn two rows in front
hidden by a shaft of earnest placard

strain to taste sunburn   stretch
(who's to know if this will be a remember?)

whiplash stop and suddenly profile
fingers
cigarette
fingers gone then another finger
piece of tobacco from lip
moving again *when do we want it*
back of neck again leaks into view
forward   crane my neck
now

want then
wanted it then
want it then and now and then

This Is Just to Say

This
is just to say
I have eaten
the plums

that were tired
from waiting
for one
of your breakfasts

Over-ripe
and flabby
they were so cold
and refreshing

I had to eat them
with a spoon
wipe the nectar
off the floor

And I feel
foolish to say
that I am
so sorry

dizzy
with grief
I can't bear it
they're gone

Hospital Visit

In the Maze below clichés spill over the deserted
street: Gestapo sirens splitting the ringing,
bouncing sexual cash registers, packaged so
tightly, like so many little moans.

There is a heady smell down there. Fear and sin
and gasoline, and the blood in the mouth taste of
war.

And I sit while this thing has got me by the hair—
with you beside me naked as a chicken foot. I must
prepare. (Herr Doktor, Herr Lucifer is here: every
touch a bribe, every word so expensive.)

I place you in your white quiver and draw you
against me. I wonder at the gravity of my
predicament and look down at my useless palms:
saturated rags. And you are burning up, your
body as dry as anger. I cover you with my hands,
I'll become your sweat.

It's time, and just as well, to re-arrange this anal-
ogy. If only until the morning. Even without
help, a July morning can kill.

Early Dinner, Week-End Away

Soft-footed summer girls enter
to light the candles at our table.

There is no magic in it.
(Were they so grim the other times?)
They wait for provocation
to return home as early as possible.

They spend each day preparing this room
wait for meal-times to claim their place
and displace them. But at the moment
it's just us and them
and a napkin mathematically angled,
pastels and the right number of glasses.
There is a balance now
which any change will spoil.

At home, I don't mind where I am.
All socks and books
I find places where the sunlight won't find me.
But the light that searches through this place
reaches me slightly green
through the bow window. I change my position.
Parachute my fingers into a less dangerous spot.
There is no way of hiding.

Upstairs, guests unclasp from their afternoon holds
they rise panting slightly, perspiring
shivering as their too-hot skin
meets the cool afternoon, withdrawing
stretching themselves in the too-loud rasp
of ice cream coloured sheets.
Soon they will descend and blush, their feet
making the floorboards ring.

The thrill that we are not them is gone.
I hear you cough, feel your lashes
smart, wet.

The Heat Yesterday

The heat yesterday gets a hold of my head, becomes the memory of a crown. Heat aggravates everything, bullies you into a little-less-alive. The inverse of an echo, the man you are about to become. Heat peels back the wild, gamy smell of boy, which is always there, waiting like curtains.

Heat erodes the gravelly bits that complicate your voice, that confuse the air—a constant static sound. Sound that has scored the last angry days with you, our horrible mis-stepped dance out of synch: every expression a glare, every touch a threat. And my two hands always struggling, working a pocket-sized game. Nothing I could do was right: the tiny silver balls never never in their nooks all at once in the heat yesterday.

In the heat yesterday I leave impoverished, embarrassed, feeling foolish, misspent. (As time goes into one of its own long toffee-like stretches.) I am amazed that I can leave, as if this was early emergence from an afternoon film. To turn the corner chased by so much runny yellow noise. So much that had been allowed to go on and on now, for so long now, without me.

The heat yesterday slices through today like cellophane. Today is an unused shellacked smell. And I am back again still. Still touch the complicated bones of knee that peek out from under a sheet. *"The heat yesterday ... "*. But you cannot hear me. A love song seeps out from the headphones that cup your innermost face.

Notes

1. The late film actor Sabu was "discovered" as a young boy just outside Mysore. In 1936, a crew headed by the documentary film-maker Robert Flaherty was in India scouting locations for *Elephant Boy*, an Alexander Korda production, when they came upon Sabu. He was immediately cast in the film and his acting career began. Korda went on to become an important figure in Sabu's life, using the young actor in several of his productions.

After the release and success of *Elephant Boy*, Sabu went on to act in a few British features, then went on to Hollywood. In the United States, he became a big box-office star and was featured regularly in Hollywood tabloid magazines, portrayed as a squeaky clean American immigrant teenager. He was often photographed with young starlets (escort in tow, of course) and his likes and dislikes, his love of America, and his gratefulness to his adopted country were frequently noted. When the United States joined the allied resistance during World War 2, Sabu also joined—as a pilot in the U.S. Air Force. He became a decorated war hero.

After the War, Sabu returned to Hollywood to find that there were very few parts available for him. As an adult South Asian man, he was not permitted to act as a romantic lead—it was felt that audiences wouldn't accept this. Parts were offered to him less and less frequently. The films in which he did appear were lower and lower grade B-pictures. There was the odd exception—*Black Narcissus*, in 1946, for which he went back to England just after the War, and *Pardon My Trunk* for Vittorio deSica in 1952 being the most notable—but for the most part Sabu's career was in decline. His biggest film successes—*Thief of Baghdad, Jungle Book,* and *Elephant Boy*—had all taken place when he was or could still pass as a child.

Acknowledgements

Several of these poems have been published—some of them in slightly different form—in *Absinthe, ARC, Bazaar, Blind Date, Border/Lines, Canadian Literature, Poetry Review, Rungh, Toronto South Asian Review, Wasafiri, West Coast Line, A Lotus of Another Colour* (Boston: Alyson), and *Beyond Destination* (Ikon: Birmingham). The long poem "Song of Sabu" was published initially as a chapbook by Disorientation Chapbooks (Calgary: 1993).

Three poems from an earlier collection, *Black Markets, White Boyfriends*, have been transplanted to this volume. "Another Country", "A Pass to India" and "Hospital Visit" are included here in new incarnations, giving direction and shape to a collection which, in many ways, they have generated.

The poem "Bastards of the Diaspora" was inspired by Himani Bannerji's essay, "Truant in Time", published in *Beyond Destination*, an exhibition catalogue published by Ikon Gallery in Birmingham, England

I'm grateful to the organisers of the 1993 Crow's Nest Pass Writing Workshop, where several of these poems were developed. I'm particularly indebted to Fred Wah and Ashok Mathur for their comments and support at the Workshop and beyond. And I'd like to offer a rather overdue thank you to Dionne Brand for her kind words and encouragement.

I'd also like to acknowledge the financial assistance of the Canada Council and the Ontario Arts Council through the Writers' Reserve Program.

Finally I'd like to thank my editor Michael Redhill, for his sharp eye and generous criticism.

About the Author

Ian Iqbal Rashid was born in Dar-Es-Salaam in 1965, raised in Toronto, and has been dividing his time between Canada and London since 1991.

The Heat Yesterday is his third poetry publication. *Black Markets, White Boyfriends and Other Acts of Elision*, (TSAR: Toronto), which was nominated for Canada's Gerald Lampert Prize, was published in 1992. *Song of Sabu*, (disOrientation: Calgary, 1993) based on the life of the late film-star Sabu, was recently published as an image-text chapbook.

His feature length screenplay, *Good Enough for Cary* will be produced in 1996 by BBC's Black Screen and the Canadian Broadcasting Corporation (CBC). Several other film and television projects are in development including *The Colour of Words*, a series of experimental films using Canadian poetry.

Rashid is a creative and critical writer who has been published by many magazines and journals in the UK and in North America. He also reviews literature and film regularly for the British Broadcasting Corporation (BBC) Radio 4's *Kaleidoscope*.